PIANO · VOCAL · GUITAR

# THE BEST PRAISE & WORSHIP SONGS EVER

WITHDRAWN

ISBN 978-0-634-06791-4

HAL•LEONARD®
CORPORATION

7777 W. BLUEMOUND RD. P.O. BOX 13819 MILWAUKEE, WI 53213

Visit Hal Leonard Online at
**www.halleonard.com**

# CONTENTS

# ABOVE ALL

Words and Music by PAUL BALOCHE
and LENNY LeBLANC

5

# AGNUS DEI

Words and Music by
MICHAEL W. SMITH

# ALL THINGS ARE POSSIBLE

Words and Music by
DARLENE ZSCHECH

# ANCIENT OF DAYS

Words and Music by GARY SADLER
and JAMIE HARVILL

# BETTER IS ONE DAY

Words and Music by
MATT REDMAN

# AS THE DEER

Words and Music by
MARTIN NYSTROM

# AWESOME GOD

Words and Music by
RICH MULLINS

**Powerfully, in 2**

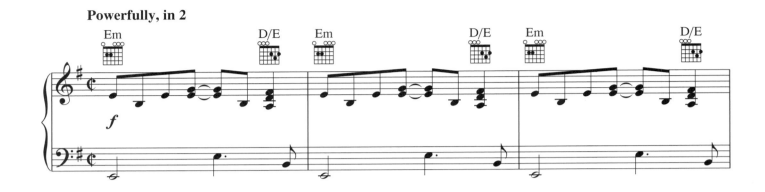

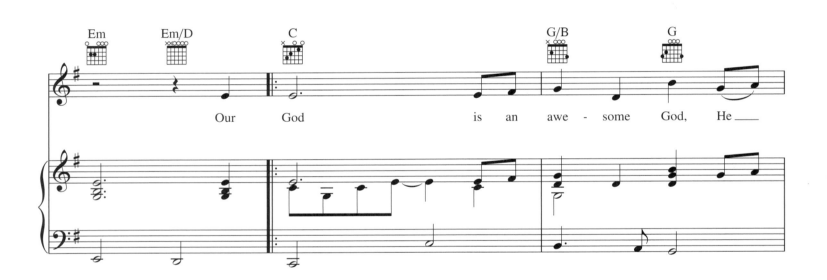

Our God is an awe-some God, He

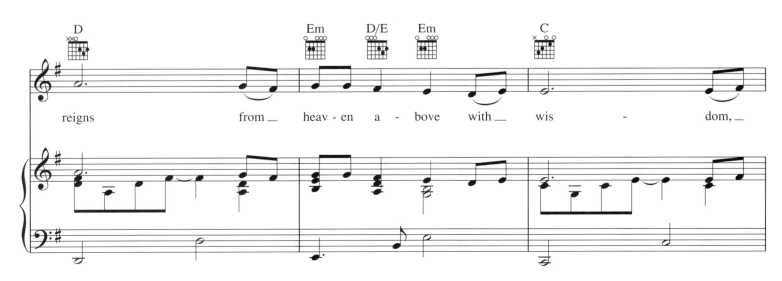

reigns from heav-en a-bove with wis - dom,

pow'r and love. Our \_\_ God is an awe - some God! Our

God! Our God is an awe - some God! Our

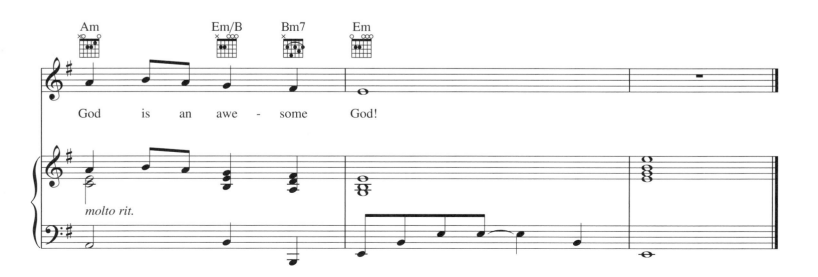

God is an awe - some God!

*molto rit.*

# BE GLORIFIED

Words and Music by LOUIE GIGLIO
and CHRIS TOMLIN

# BE UNTO YOUR NAME

Words and Music by LYNN DeSHAZO
and GARY SADLER

# BREATHE

Words and Music by
MARIE BARNETT

**With emotion**

# CELEBRATE JESUS

Words and Music by
GARY OLIVER

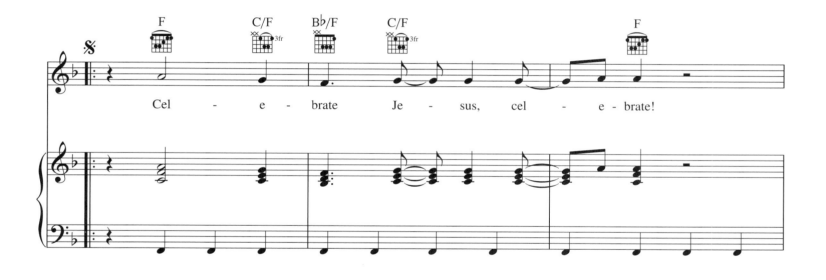

Cel - e - brate Je - sus, cel - e - brate!

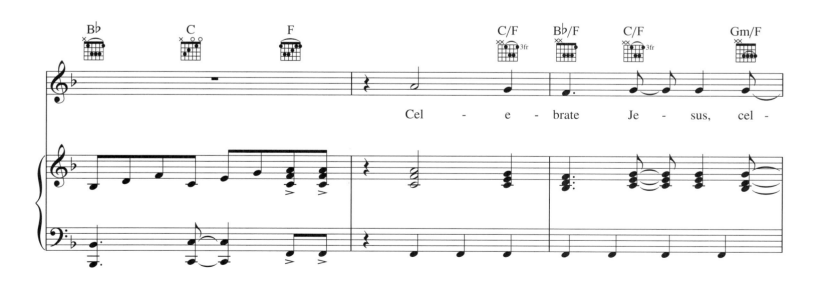

Cel - e - brate Je - sus, cel -

# CHANGE MY HEART OH GOD

Words and Music by
EDDIE ESPINOSA

43

# COME INTO HIS PRESENCE

Words and Music by
LYNN BAIRD

# COME, NOW IS THE TIME TO WORSHIP

Words and Music by
BRIAN DOERKSEN

Come, ... now is the time __ to wor -

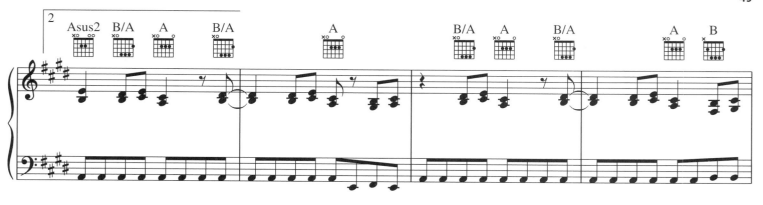

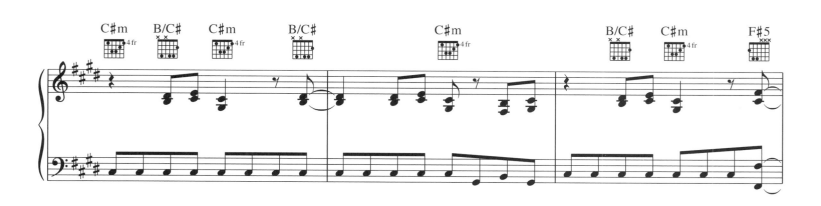

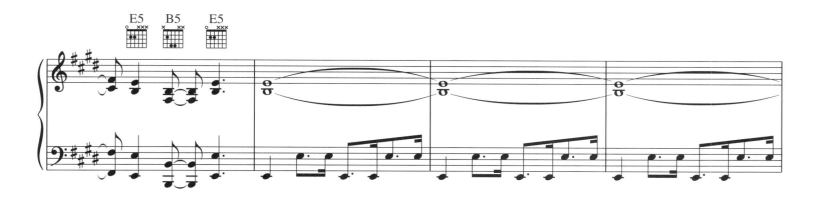

Ooh, _____

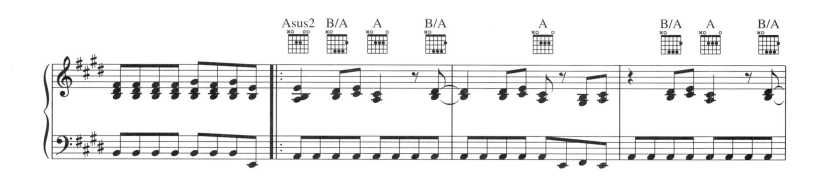

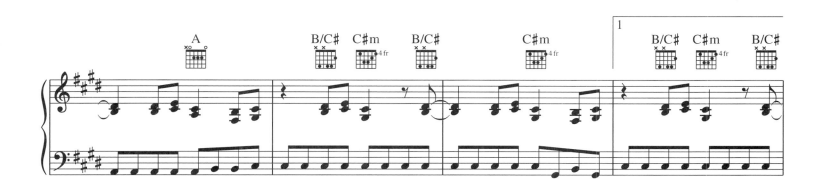

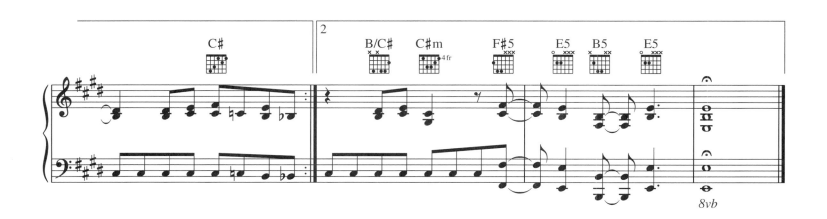

# CREATE IN ME A CLEAN HEART

Words and Music by
KEITH GREEN

# CRY OF MY HEART

Words and Music by
TERRY BUTLER

# DAYS OF ELIJAH

Words and Music by
ROBIN MARK

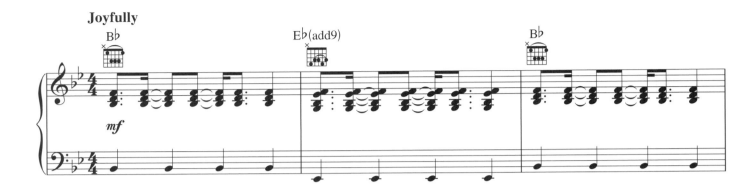

These are __ the days of __ E-
these are __ the days of __ E-

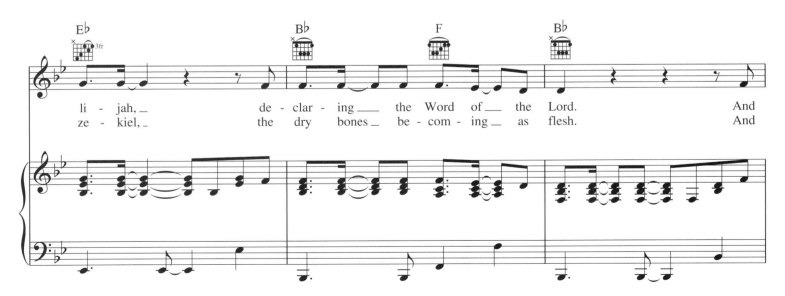

li - jah, __ de - clar - ing __ the Word of __ the Lord. And
ze - kiel, __ the dry bones __ be - com - ing __ as flesh. And

# DID YOU FEEL THE MOUNTAINS TREMBLE?

Words and Music by
MARTIN SMITH

64

# DRAW ME CLOSE

Words and Music by
KELLY CARPENTER

# FIRM FOUNDATION

Words and Music by NANCY GORDON
and JAMIE HARVILL

# ENOUGH

Words and Music by CHRIS TOMLIN
and LOUIE GIGLIO

# EVERY MOVE I MAKE

Words and Music by
DAVID RUIS

# FOREVER

Words and Music by
CHRIS TOMLIN

# GIVE THANKS

Words and Music by
HENRY SMITH

# GLORIFY THY NAME

Words and Music by
DONNA ADKINS

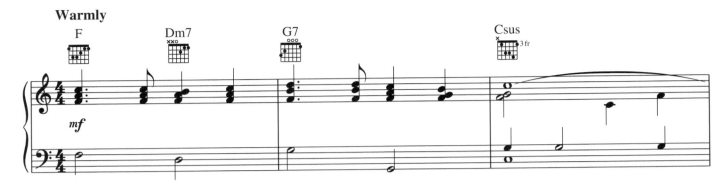

Fa - ther, we love You, we
Je - sus, we love You, we
Spir - it, we love You, we

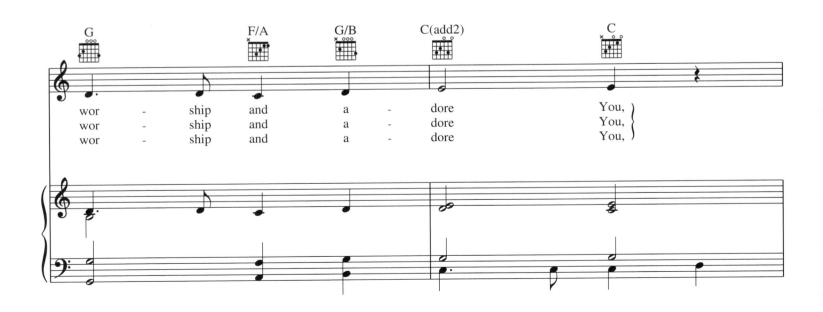

wor - ship and a - dore You,
wor - ship and a - dore You,
wor - ship and a - dore You,

# GREAT IS THE LORD

Words and Music by MICHAEL W. SMITH
and DEBORAH D. SMITH

**Brightly, flowing**

Great is the Lord, He is ho - ly and just; by His

pow - er we trust in His love. _____ Great is the Lord, He is

faith - ful and true; by His mer - cy He proves He is love. _____

94

# GOD IS GOOD ALL THE TIME

Words and Music by DON MOEN
and PAUL OVERSTREET

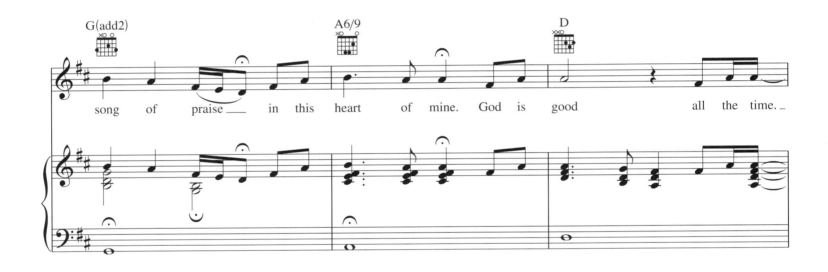

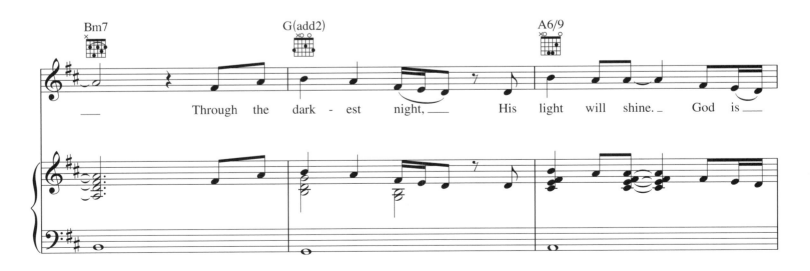

# GOD OF WONDERS

Words and Music by MARC BYRD
and STEVE HINDALONG

Lord of all ___ cre-a-tion, ___
Ear-ly in ___ the morn-ing ___

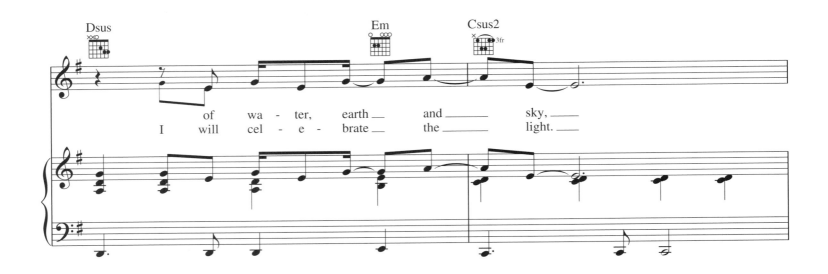

of wa-ter, earth ___ and ___ sky, ___
I will cel-e-brate ___ the ___ light. ___

the heav-ens are Your tab-er-na-cle; ___
And as I stum-ble in the dark-ness, ___

# HALLELUJAH
## (Your Love Is Amazing)

Words and Music by BRENTON BROWN
and BRIAN DOERKSEN

Joyfully

(1., 3.) Your love is ___ a-maz ___ -ing, stead-y and ___ un-chang ___ -ing. Your love is ___ a moun-
(2.) ___ -ing, I can feel ___ it ris ___ -ing, all the joy ___ that's grow-

- tain, firm be-neath ___ my feet. ___ Your love is ___ a mys-
- ing deep in-side ___ of me. ___ And ev-'ry time ___ I see ___

- t'ry, how You gen-tly lift _____ me when I am ___ sur-round-
___ You, all Your good ___ -ness shines _____ through, and I can feel ___ this God

# HE HAS MADE ME GLAD

By LEONA VON BRETHORST

# HE IS EXALTED

Words and Music by
TWILA PARIS

# THE HEART OF WORSHIP

Words and Music by
MATT REDMAN

# HERE I AM TO WORSHIP

Words and Music by
TIM HUGHES

**Moderately slow**

Light of the World, You stepped down in-to dark-ness,
King of all days, oh so high-ly ex-alt-ed,

o-pened my eyes, let me ____ see. ____
glo-rious in heav-en a - bove. ____

Beau-ty that made this ____
Hum-bly You came to the

heart a - dore ____ You, hope of a life spent with ____ You. ____
earth You cre-a-ted, all for love's sake be-came ____ poor. ____

er know_ how much_ it cost_ to see_ my sin_ up - on_

_ that cross._ And I'll nev-_ that cross._ Here I am to

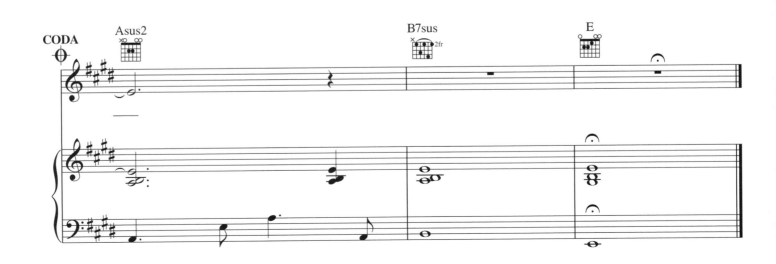

# HERE WE ARE

Words and Music by DON MOEN
and CLAIRE CLONINGER

Moderately slow

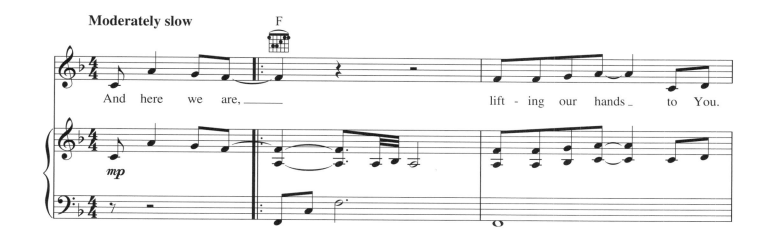

And here we are, \_\_\_\_\_ lift-ing our hands \_ to You.

Here \_ we are, _____

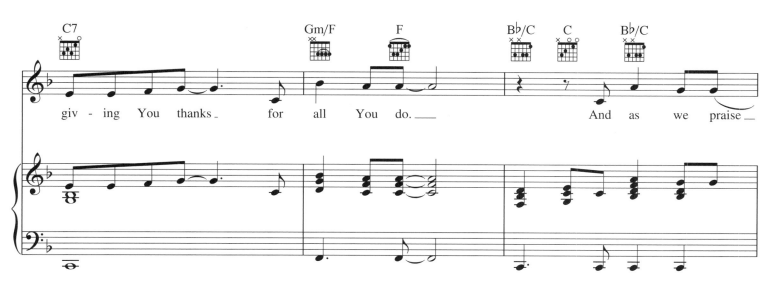

giv-ing You thanks \_ for all You do. \_\_\_ And as we praise \_

128

# HOLINESS

Words and Music by
SCOTT UNDERWOOD

# I COULD SING OF YOUR LOVE FOREVER

Words and Music by
MARTIN SMITH

Female: La la la___ la la___ la la___

___ la la.

# HOLY AND ANOINTED ONE

Words and Music by
JOHN BARNETT

# HOW MAJESTIC IS YOUR NAME

Words and Music by
MICHAEL W. SMITH

Lord, _ our Lord, _ how ma-jes-tic is Your name _ in all _____ the ___

149

# I GIVE YOU MY HEART

Words and Music by
REUBEN MORGAN

This is my ___ de-si-re, ___ to hon - or ___

# I LOVE YOU LORD

Words and Music by
LAURIE KLEIN

Am7 C7 F B♭/F
soul, re - joice! Take joy, my King,
F C/F F F7
in what You hear.
May it be a
B♭ F/C C7
sweet, sweet sound in Your
1
F Dm F/C
ear.
B♭ C7
I
2
F Dm F/C B♭m B♭m6 F
ear.
6 fr
rit.

# I OFFER MY LIFE

Words and Music by DON MOEN
and CLAIRE CLONINGER

Lord, I of - fer my life ___ to You. Ev - 'ry - thing I've ___ been through, ___

# IT IS YOU

Words and Music by
PETER FURLER

Moderately slow

As we lift up our hands, ____ will You meet us here? ____ As we call on Your name, _

____ will You meet us here? ____ We have come to this place ____ to wor - ship You, _

____ God of mer - cy and grace. ____ It is You ____ we a - dore. _

# I STAND IN AWE

Words and Music by
MARK ALTROGGE

# I WANT TO BE WHERE YOU ARE

Words and Music by
DON MOEN

# I WANT TO KNOW YOU

Words and Music by
ANDY PARK

# I WORSHIP YOU, ALMIGHTY GOD

Words and Music by
SONDRA CORBETT-WOOD

# JESUS, LOVER OF MY SOUL

Words and Music by JOHN EZZY,
DANIEL GRUL and STEPHEN McPHERSON

# JESUS, NAME ABOVE ALL NAMES

Words and Music by
NAIDA HEARN

# KNOWING YOU
## (All I Once Held Dear)

Words and Music by
GRAHAM KENDRICK

Worshipfully

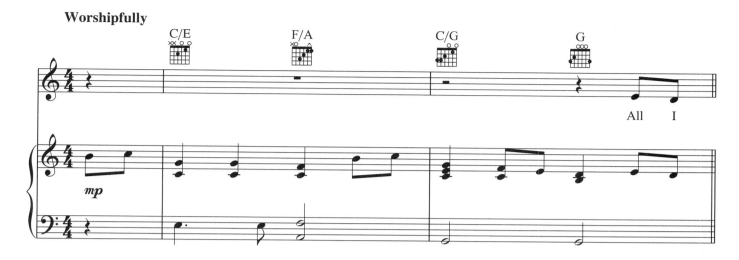

All I
once held dear, built my life up - on, all this world re - veres and
heart's de - sire is to know You more, to be found in You and
know the pow'r of Your ris - en life and to know You in Your

wars to own,
known as Yours,
suf - fer - ings,

all I once thought gain I have
to pos - sess by faith what I
to be - come like You in Your

count - ed ____ loss, spent and worth - less ____ now com - pared to
could not ____ earn, all - sur - pass - ing ____ gift of right - eous -
death, my ____ Lord, so with You to ____ live and nev - er

this: }
ness. } Know-ing You, Je - sus, know - ing You; there
die. }

is no great - er thing. You're my all, You're the best,___ You're my

joy, my right-eous-ness, __ and I love You, Lord. _____

{ Now my
{ Oh, to love You, Lord. _____ And I

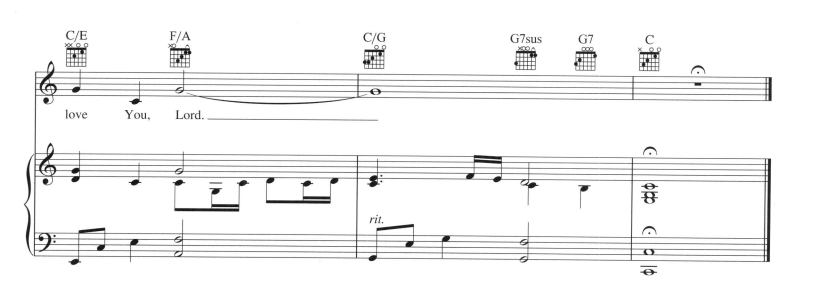

love You, Lord. _____

# LAMB OF GOD

Words and Music by
TWILA PARIS

# LET EVERYTHING THAT HAS BREATH

Words and Music by
MATT REDMAN

# LORD, I LIFT YOUR NAME ON HIGH

Words and Music by
RICK FOUNDS

197

# LORD HAVE MERCY

Words and Music by
STEVE MERKEL

Lord have mer - cy on ____ me. me.

D.S. al Coda

CODA

# LORD, REIGN IN ME

Words and Music by
BRENTON BROWN

204

# MAJESTY

Words and Music by
JACK W. HAYFORD

# MIGHTY IS OUR GOD

Words and Music by EUGENE GRECO,
GERRIT GUSTAFSON and DON MOEN

# MORE LOVE, MORE POWER

Words and Music by
JUDE DEL HIERRO

Lyrics:
More love, — more pow-er, more of You — in my ____ life. More love, — more pow-er, more of You — in my ____ life. And I will wor-ship

# MORE PRECIOUS THAN SILVER

Words and Music by
LYNN DeSHAZO

Lord,          You are          more pre - cious          than

sil - ver.          Lord,          You are          more

# MY LIFE IS IN YOU, LORD

Words and Music by
DANIEL GARDNER

219

# MY REDEEMER LIVES

Words and Music by
REUBEN MORGAN

I be - lieve. __

My shame He's tak - en a - way. __

My pain is healed in His name. I be - lieve, __

# NO OTHER NAME

Words and Music by
ROBERT GAY

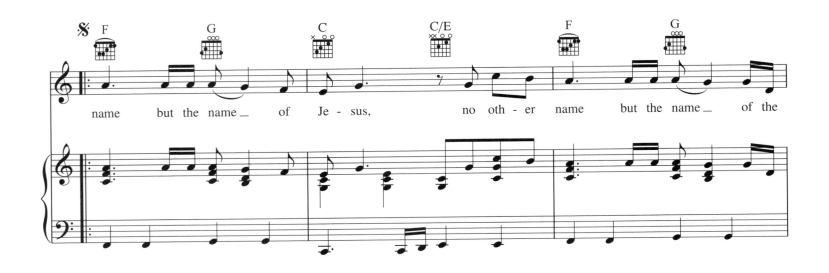

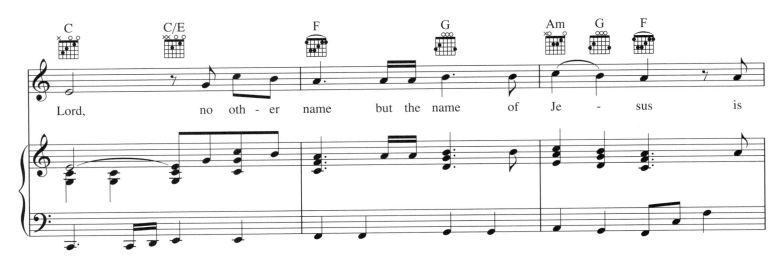

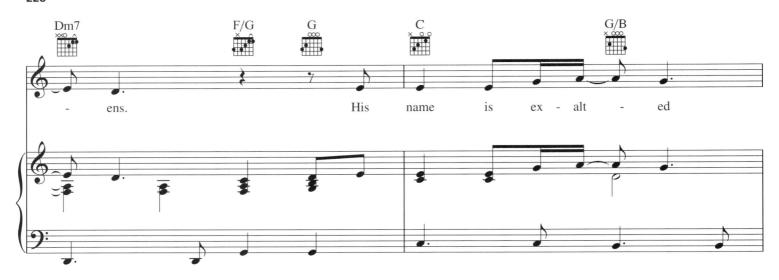

His name is ex - alt - ed

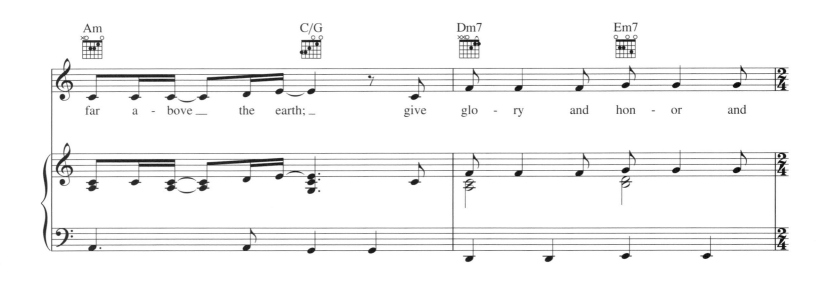

far a - bove the earth; give glo - ry and hon - or and

**D.S. al Coda**
**(with repeat)**

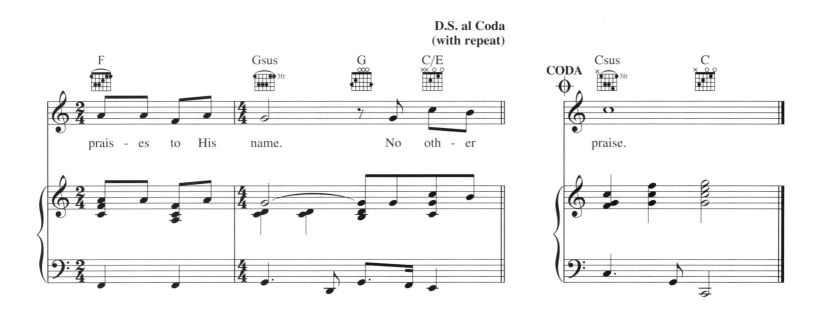

prais - es to His name. No oth - er praise.

# OH LORD, YOU'RE BEAUTIFUL

Words and Music by
KEITH GREEN

# OPEN THE EYES OF MY HEART

Words and Music by
PAUL BALOCHE

240

# THE POTTER'S HAND

Words and Music by
DARLENE ZSCHECH

# REFINER'S FIRE

Words and Music by
BRIAN DOERKSEN

# SANCTUARY

Words and Music by JOHN THOMPSON
and RANDY SCRUGGS

**Moderately slow**

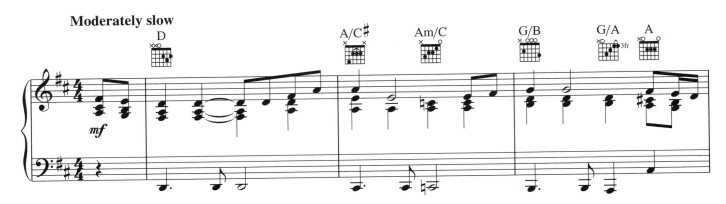

Lord, pre- pare me _____ to be a sanc- tu- ar- y, pure and

ho- ly, tried and true. _____ With thanks- giv- ing, I'll be a

# SHINE, JESUS, SHINE

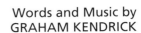

Words and Music by
GRAHAM KENDRICK

**With excitement**

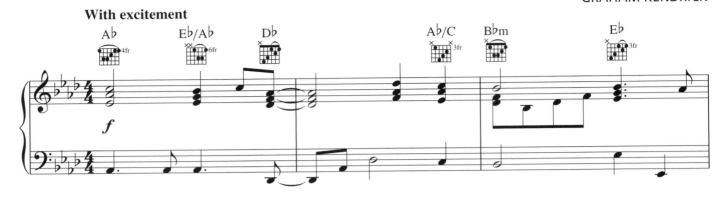

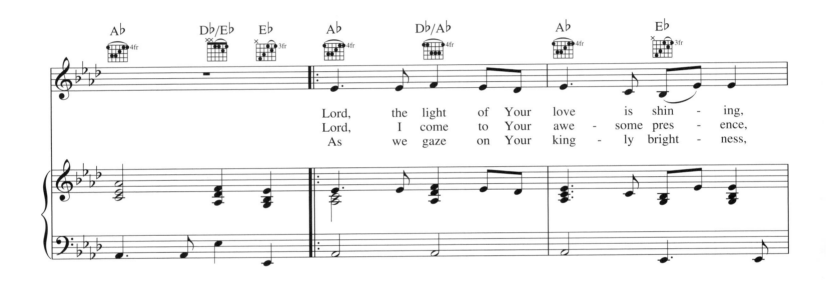

Lord,     the light   of  Your  love     is shin - ing,
Lord,     I come   to   Your  awe - some pres - ence,
As     we gaze   on   Your  king - ly bright - ness,

in     the midst   of  the   dark - ness shin - ing.   Je - sus,   Light  of  the
from   the shad - ows   in - to   Your  ra - diance.   By   the   blood  I  may
so     our fac - es   dis - play   Your  like - ness.   Ev - er   chang - ing  from

set our hearts on fire.

Flow, riv - er, flow, ___ flood the na - tions with

grace and mer - cy. Send forth Your Word, ___ Lord, and

let there be light. light.

# SHINE ON US

Words and Music by MICHAEL W. SMITH
and DEBBIE SMITH

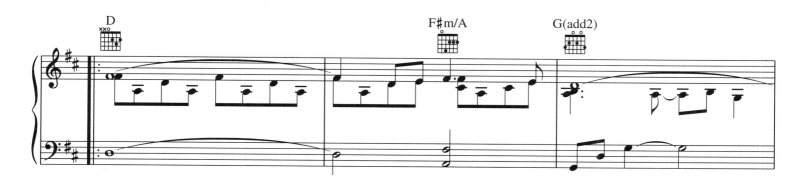

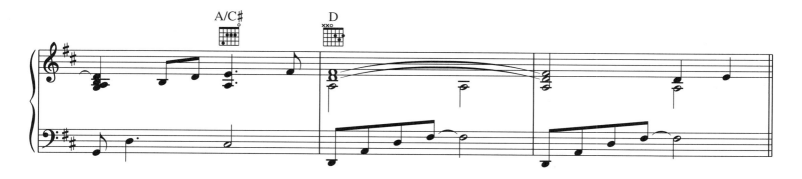

Lord, _____ let your light,
Lord, _____ let your grace,

# SHOUT TO THE LORD

Words and Music by
DARLENE ZSCHECH

# STEP BY STEP

Words and Music by
DAVID STRASSER "BEAKER"

265

# THERE IS A REDEEMER

Words and Music by
MELODY GREEN

**Moderately**

1. There    is    a    re  -  deem  -  er,
2.-4. *(See additional lyrics)*

Je  -  sus,    God's    own    Son.

Spir - it till the work on earth is done.

CODA

done. And leav - ing Your Spir - it till the

work _ on _ earth _ is done.

*Additional Lyrics*

2. Jesus, my redeemer,
   Name above all names.
   Precious Lamb of God, Messiah,
   Oh, for sinners slain. *(To Chorus)*

3. When I stand in glory,
   I will see His face,
   And there I'll serve my King forever
   In that holy place. *(To Chorus)*

4. There is a redeemer,
   Jesus, God's own Son.
   Precious Lamb of God, Messiah,
   Holy One. *(To Chorus)*

# WE BOW DOWN

Words and Music by
TWILA PARIS

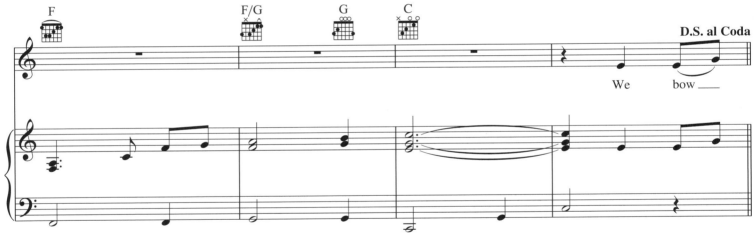

We bow ___

D.S. al Coda

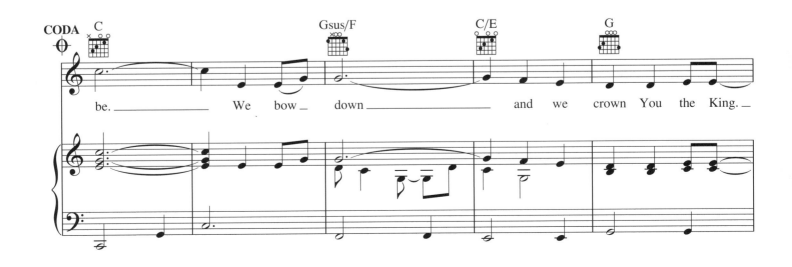

be. _____ We bow _ down _____ and we crown You the King. __

# THIS IS THE DAY

By LES GARRETT

**Joyfully**

This is the day, this is the day that the Lord has made, that the Lord has made.

I will re-joice, I will re-joice and be

# TRADING MY SORROWS

Words and Music by
DARRELL EVANS

277

# WE FALL DOWN

Words and Music by
CHRIS TOMLIN

# WE WILL GLORIFY

Words and Music by
TWILA PARIS

# YOU ARE MY KING
## (Amazing Love)

Words and Music by
BILLY JAMES FOOTE

I'm for-giv - en ____ be - cause You were _ for - sak - en.

I'm ac - cept - ed; You were _ con - demned. _ I'm a - live _ and well; _ Your

Spir - it is ____ with - in ____ me be - cause You died ____ and rose _ a - gain. ____

# WORTHY, YOU ARE WORTHY

Words and Music by
DON MOEN

# YOU ARE HOLY
## (Prince of Peace)

Words and Music by MARC IMBODEN
and TAMMI RHOTON

# YOU ARE SO GOOD TO ME

Words and Music by DON CHAFFER,
BEN PASLEY and ROBIN PASLEY

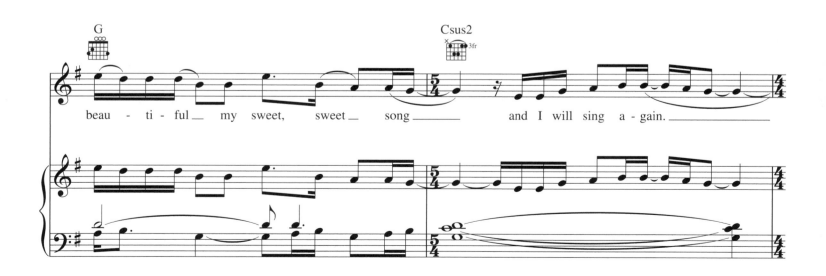

# THE BEST EVER COLLECTION

## ARRANGED FOR PIANO, VOICE AND GUITAR

### 150 of the Most Beautiful Songs Ever
150 ballads: Bewitched • (They Long to Be) Close to You • How Deep Is Your Love • I'll Be Seeing You • Unchained Melody • Yesterday • Young at Heart • more.
00360735 ................................................................ $22.95

### Best Acoustic Rock Songs Ever
65 acoustic hits: Dust in the Wind • Fast Car • I Will Remember You • Landslide • Leaving on a Jet Plane • Maggie May • Tears in Heaven • Yesterday • more.
00310984 ................................................................ $19.95

### Best Big Band Songs Ever
Over 60 big band hits: Boogie Woogie Bugle Boy • Don't Get Around Much Anymore • In the Mood • Moonglow • Sentimental Journey • Who's Sorry Now • more.
00359129 ................................................................ $16.95

### Best Broadway Songs Ever
Over 70 songs in all! Includes: All I Ask of You • Bess, You Is My Woman • Climb Ev'ry Mountain • Comedy Tonight • If I Were a Rich Man • Ol' Man River • more!
00309155 ................................................................ $20.95

### Best Children's Songs Ever
Over 100 songs: Bingo • Eensy Weensy Spider • The Farmer in the Dell • On Top of Spaghetti • Puff the Magic Dragon • Twinkle, Twinkle Little Star • and more.
00310360 (Easy Piano) ..................................... $19.95

### Best Christmas Songs Ever
More than 60 holiday favorites: Frosty the Snow Man • A Holly Jolly Christmas • I'll Be Home for Christmas • Rudolph, The Red-Nosed Reindeer • Silver Bells • more.
00359130 ................................................................ $19.95

### Best Classic Rock Songs Ever
Over 60 hits: American Woman • Bang a Gong • Cold As Ice • Heartache Tonight • Rock and Roll All Nite • Smoke on the Water • Wonderful Tonight • and more.
00310800 ................................................................ $18.95

### Best Classical Music Ever
Over 80 of classical favorites: Ave Maria • Canon in D • Eine Kleine Nachtmusik • Für Elise • Lacrymosa • Ode to Joy • William Tell Overture • and many more.
00310674 ................................................................ $19.95

### Best Contemporary Christian Songs Ever
Over 70 favorites, including: Awesome God • El Shaddai • Friends • Jesus Freak • People Need the Lord • Place in This World • Serve the Lord • Thy Word • more.
00310558 ................................................................ $19.95

### Best Country Songs Ever
78 classic country hits: Always on My Mind • Crazy • Daddy Sang Bass • Forever and Ever, Amen • God Bless the U.S.A. • I Fall to Pieces • Through the Years • more.
00359135 ................................................................ $17.95

### Best Early Rock N Roll Songs Ever
Over 70 songs, including: Book of Love • Crying • Do Wah Diddy Diddy • Louie, Louie • Peggy Sue • Shout • Splish Splash • Stand By Me • Tequila • and more.
00310816 ................................................................ $17.95

### Best Easy Listening Songs Ever
75 mellow favorites: (They Long to Be) Close to You • Every Breath You Take • How Am I Supposed to Live Without You • Unchained Melody • more.
00359193 ................................................................ $18.95

### Best Gospel Songs Ever
80 gospel songs: Amazing Grace • Daddy Sang Bass • How Great Thou Art • I'll Fly Away • Just a Closer Walk with Thee • The Old Rugged Cross • more.
00310503 ................................................................ $19.95

### Best Hymns Ever
118 hymns: Abide with Me • Every Time I Feel the Spirit • He Leadeth Me • I Love to Tell the Story • Were You There? • When I Survey the Wondrous Cross • and more.
00310774 ................................................................ $17.95

### Best Jazz Standards Ever
77 jazz hits: April in Paris • Don't Get Around Much Anymore • Love Is Here to Stay • Misty • Satin Doll • Unforgettable • When I Fall in Love • and more.
00311641 ................................................................ $19.95

### More of the Best Jazz Standards Ever
74 beloved jazz hits: Ain't Misbehavin' • Blue Skies • Come Fly with Me • Honeysuckle Rose • The Lady Is a Tramp • Moon River • My Funny Valentine • and more.
00311023 ................................................................ $19.95

### Best Latin Songs Ever
67 songs: Besame Mucho (Kiss Me Much) • The Girl from Ipanema • Malaguena • Slightly Out of Tune (Desafinado) • Summer Samba (So Nice) • and more.
00310355 ................................................................ $19.95

### Best Love Songs Ever
65 favorite love songs, including: Endless Love • Here and Now • Love Takes Time • Misty • My Funny Valentine • So in Love • You Needed Me • Your Song.
00359198 ................................................................ $19.95

### Best Movie Songs Ever
74 songs from the movies: Almost Paradise • Chariots of Fire • My Heart Will Go On • Take My Breath Away • Unchained Melody • You'll Be in My Heart • more.
00310063 ................................................................ $19.95

### Best R&B Songs Ever
66 songs, including: Baby Love • Endless Love • Here and Now • I Will Survive • Saving All My Love for You • Stand By Me • What's Going On • and more.
00310184 ................................................................ $19.95

### Best Rock Songs Ever
Over 60 songs: All Shook Up • Blue Suede Shoes • Born to Be Wild • Every Breath You Take • Free Bird • Hey Jude • We Got the Beat • Wild Thing • more!
00490424 ................................................................ $18.95

### Best Songs Ever
Over 70 must-own classics: Edelweiss • Love Me Tender • Memory • My Funny Valentine • Tears in Heaven • Unforgettable • A Whole New World • and more.
00359224 ................................................................ $22.95

### More of the Best Songs Ever
79 more favorites: April in Paris • Candle in the Wind • Endless Love • Misty • My Blue Heaven • My Heart Will Go On • Stella by Starlight • Witchcraft • more.
00310437 ................................................................ $19.95

### Best Standards Ever, Vol. 1 (A-L)
72 beautiful ballads, including: All the Things You Are • Bewitched • God Bless' the Child • I've Got You Under My Skin • The Lady Is a Tramp • more.
00359231 ................................................................ $16.95

### Best Standards Ever, Vol. 2 (M-Z)
72 songs: Makin' Whoopee • Misty • My Funny Valentine • People Will Say We're in Love • Smoke Gets in Your Eyes • Strangers in the Night • Tuxedo Junction • more.
00359232 ................................................................ $16.95

### More of the Best Standards Ever, Vol. 1 (A-L)
76 all-time favorites: Ain't Misbehavin' • Always • Autumn in New York • Desafinado • Fever • Fly Me to the Moon • Georgia on My Mind • and more.
00310813 ................................................................ $17.95

### More of the Best Standards Ever, Vol. 2 (M-Z)
75 more stunning standards: Mona Lisa • Mood Indigo • Moon River • Norwegian Wood • Route 66 • Sentimental Journey • Stella by Starlight • What'll I Do? • and more.
00310814 ................................................................ $17.95

### Best Torch Songs Ever
70 sad and sultry favorites: All by Myself • Crazy • Fever • I Will Remember You • Misty • Stormy Weather (Keeps Rainin' All the Time) • Unchained Melody • and more.
00311027 ................................................................ $19.95

### Best TV Songs Ever
Over 50 fun and catchy theme songs: The Addams Family • The Brady Bunch • Happy Days • Mission: Impossible • Where Everybody Knows Your Name • and more!
00311048 ................................................................ $17.95

FOR MORE INFORMATION, SEE YOUR LOCAL MUSIC DEALER, OR WRITE TO:

HAL•LEONARD CORPORATION
7777 W. BLUEMOUND RD. P.O. BOX 13819 MILWAUKEE, WI 53213

Visit us on-line for complete songlists at
**www.halleonard.com**